Are You Ready For True Love?

Assessing Relational Compatibility & Responsibility

By Paul Davis

Copyright © 2007 by Paul Davis

Are You Ready For True Love?
by Paul Davis

Printed in the United States of America

ISBN-13: 978-1-60034-901-0
ISBN-10: 1-60034-901-3

All rights reserved solely by the author. The author guarantees all contents are original and do not infringe upon the legal rights of any other person or work. No part of this book may be reproduced in any form without the permission of the author. The views expressed in this book are not necessarily those of the publisher.

Unless otherwise indicated, Bible quotations are taken from the King James Version from biblegateway.com.

Cover design by Chris Johnson
Image Idea by Karla Ruzycki Davis

www.xulonpress.com

Acknowledgments

Thanks to my wife Karla for helping me understand and experience true love. Your unconditional love and faithful support strengthen me personally whereby I can have a strong foundation from which to impact the nations. Thanks for bringing a new world order to our house, whereby our home can be a place where heaven can come to earth. You are an amazing wife, helper and lifelong companion.

Thanks to my mother and father, Paul and Paulette Davis, for their steadfast love through every season of my life. Your marriage of over thirty years has shown me what it is to rejoice and happily live together. Thanks for all your love and laughs we have shared together.

Thanks to all my friends throughout the world who have shared your hearts, lives, and stories with me. Your transparency and trust has greatly enlightened me whereby I have grown personally and can through this book help humanity.

Thanks to Roberto LoPresti and Chris Johnson for their wonderful friendship, outstanding work, and commitment to excellence. Your web design, videograpy, graphic artisty, and creativity have enabled me to communicate my messages powerfully visually and globally.

Thanks to my Creator who has imparted the spirit of love to my heart whereby I can know true unconditional love experientially, articulate it wisely, and impart it powerfully.

Table of Contents

1. Discover Higher Dimensions............................13
2. Explore and Evaluate Identity..........................19
3. Consider Core Values......................................33
4. Identify Beliefs...47
5. Assess Mental Models & Mindsets...................63
6. Examine Behavior..71
7. Evaluate Environmental Issues........................85

Introduction

"I just want true love." This is what the lovely young lady with whom I was having lunch told me. I replied: "You're not ready for true love!" She was utterly shocked I could say such a thing and undoubtedly offended. "You are cruel." She told me.

"No, it is you who are cruel Lena. You continue to date a guy who you don't love. You have repeatedly broken up with him. You say you cannot leave him, but yet you date other guys on the side while you are with him. You are not ready for true love because you are not ready for truth. Truth precedes true love. You cannot have 'true love' without first embracing truth. You are living a lie and lying to yourself."

Upon entering this dialogue and exchange of words, I immediately knew within that I must write a book on this topic. Clear across the world in Odessa, Ukraine I got a full glimpse of just how many people play one another relationally while waiting for something "better" to come along. Perhaps you have been on the other end of being "played" yourself and did not recognize what was going on. Well let me help you alleviate the confusion and position you to now see more clearly what is in front of you.

Since part of my academic training is in lie detection and interrogation, I have become increasingly discerning on a relational level. Thankfully I heard enough from Lena to realize I did not want to befriend such a person, not to mention consider dating her. Though she portrayed herself as a single woman, it was obvious that she had commitments elsewhere and therefore was double-minded everywhere. Her inability to commit was the root cause of her continual confusion. Yet somewhere deep within I sensed that she liked to play "the damsel in distress" role so as to get additional attention from the male gender. To her surprise I both saw through it and would have no part in it.

The games people play relationally are many. Yet there still are some sincere souls in the world who genuinely want to embrace truth, find love and be happy in a meaningful relationship. It just takes some time to find such people and sort through all the others who are incongruent and unable to determine what they ultimately desire.

Isn't that basically the problem? We don't know what we want. Therefore we often vacillate in indecision, devaluing and torturing those around us who love us most. Thankfully for those we make suffer, most eventually come to their senses and move on leaving us to sort out ourselves. It is exhausting trying to put your finger on a person's problem and help them through it when they themselves haven't determined truly what the problem is.

Yet such incongruence and lack of personal integration can easily be seen upon a person's face.

It almost looks like Harrison Ford's prized half confused, half angry look. Such intense bewilderment leads to internal frustration, which outwardly eventually lashes out against those around them with anger. The root of the problem is simply an unresolved matter of the heart.

As such a person continually maintains this deep pondering look on their face, their eyes glazed over, their mind journeying to another destination, not fully present, they try to sort out their internal unfinished business.

Have you ever been there? I'm sure we all have. I am also sure you have had the opportunity, like it or not, of interacting with such a person. The tell-all clue is they are present in body with you but absent in mind.

As it pertains to relationships and love, it can be a very unique creature to dissect and understand. The parts I have observed, experienced, encountered and dealt with are from whence this book comes.

The irony is this – we all want true love, continually crave it and perpetually seek it. Yet we often sabotage it when we find it because we still haven't come to terms with what it exactly is we want. Therefore when true love comes our way we don't recognize it because we are off exploring some other land, revolving around a romance novel we read or considering the relational options elsewhere.

This book is writing me as much as I am writing it. It is the result of pressing past my emotions for answers, pursuing truth and painstakingly pondering these principles while experientially applying or omitting them in my own life. I have learned both from my mistakes and successes.

It has been said that much of your happiness in life is determined by the person who you marry. If this is so, then this book is a must read for all singles prior to selecting a future spouse.

Divorcees can learn from past mistakes and discover underlying factors motivating what they did and said when in relationships. Parents would also greatly benefit from reading this book as they prepare to counsel their children who are marriage minded.

I have intentionally not withheld my personal information within this text so as to provide living examples of what to do and what not to do. My decisions (right or wrong) at any given moment of time in the past are by no means a reflection on my current moral state or present convictions. These stories simply serve to illustrate my points and bring to life the truths expressed in this book.

Discover Higher Dimensions

Each of us are drawn to a higher system within whether we know it or not. Consciously and unconsciously there is an innate sense of destiny, which we continually reach and feel for. Many recognize and acknowledge a higher power, while others profess no belief in deity whatsoever. Perhaps you have a sense of service to your Creator, country or community. You may even be inclined to seek to serve all three.

What is most important however is that you realize your spirituality is a part of your essence. You are not a human being having a spiritual experience. You are a spiritual being having a human experience.

Whatever your religious beliefs may or may not be, the important thing is that you know your concept of the universe. Once you do, you can more easily discover the higher systems others hold dear to their hearts.

Instead of imposing your cosmic concepts on others, it is more important that you know where they are coming from so you can assess your relational compatibility. Some people are more flexible when it comes to their spiritual systems than others.

One attractive woman from the Ukraine told me, "I go to the Russian Orthodox church and I am not changing as I am happy there. I will not go to another church." Such a rigid remark immediately enabled me to eliminate her from my list of possible spouses. Not because she was a bad person. She just was not suitable for me since I am a lifelong learner and committed to spiritual growth, which requires an open mind and willingness to change.

Yet what I deem to be inflexible another person may consider a noble quality that reflects loyalty, a strong sense of self and certainty. There are no fast and hard requirements, as you alone possess the answers to these most probing questions regarding your likes and dislikes. Some seek similarities whereas others seek opposite qualities. "To each his own" as the saying goes.

Spiritual beliefs often reflect the inner essence of a person and surface at the most peculiar times. It is quite common for a couple to go on happily for years without ever assessing spiritual compatibility until their first child is born, after which they suddenly want to explore what religious beliefs to instill in their child. Of course I would strongly recommend exploring and assessing spiritual compatibility early on before you say "I do" and make a lifetime commitment to someone.

It has been said that a strong spirit is crucial to sustain a person through life's difficulties and challenges. If that is true, then our spiritual foundation should be examined and assessed to ensure we can relationally endure.

When religious activities and traditions play a significant role in a person's family, you would be wise to question just how much of this individual's religion and tradition you want to embrace after marriage. The truth of the matter is after you are married, it is very unlikely that you will change your spouse or their family.

As for me I am a born-again Christian who has been baptized and is Spirit filled and led. This does not even register nor mean anything to most people, not to mention many espousing Christians. I therefore prefer to seek someone with my spiritual background, heritage and understanding. Just any self-professed Christian will not do for me. It should be no different for you. Therefore be clear as to what you deem to be your greater system. Then unashamedly state the qualifications and ideology of the person whom you want to marry. Dare to discover the higher dimensions pertaining to one's religious beliefs.

Acknowledge your higher system's metaphorical symbols. For example when I first did this exercise, an image of a lighthouse immediately burst forth inside of me. To me a lighthouse represents a beacon of hope, direction, illumination, a navigational point and source of guidance. That lighthouse was essentially me in Christ, as a light to the world.

Key Points Review

Each of us are inwardly drawn to a higher system and Source whether we know it or not.

Consciously and unconsciously there is an innate sense of destiny, which we continually reach and feel for

You are not a human being having a spiritual experience. You are a spiritual being having a human experience.

A strong spirit is crucial to sustain a person through life's difficulties and challenges. Therefore our spiritual foundation should be examined and assessed to ensure we can relationally endure.

After you are married it is very unlikely that you will change your spouse or their family in regard to religious matters and traditions.

Questions to Ask Yourself and Others

- Define yourself spiritually?

- How important is spirituality to you?

- What higher entity if any are you indebted to?

- Do you adhere to a sense of servitude to your Creator, country or community?

- How do you define your higher power?

- What do you not adhere to in regard to spirituality or a higher power?

- What do you feel about the supernatural and miraculous?

- How much do you believe your life purpose to be intertwined with your Creator and predetermined by the divine?

- How do you differentiate between God and religion?

Explore and Evaluate Identity

The question of identity is one that philosophers throughout the ages have given attention to and deeply pondered. Identity is something many have not yet discovered concerning themselves and are still exploring.

It has been said, "It takes two to know one." In other words, you can't know yourself *by* yourself. We know ourselves in relation to others. Often it is the feedback of others who can see and kindly acknowledge our gifts that both affirm us and enable us to know who we are. The problem is when we get negative feedback from small-minded people who can't see past their nose as to our highest potential. We therefore want to be wise as to who we listen to and not allow ourselves to be pigeon-holed by another's limited mindset or miniscule ideological orbit.

Better yet is to only allow labels that enhance our identity and pull us toward becoming the people we truly desire to be rather than embracing labels that dwarf, confine and restrict us from further evolving and growing.

Identity is simply our sense of certainty about who we are. It defines our individuality and creates our world. We define ourselves not only by who we are, but also by who we are not. Identity is our most core belief about our personhood, what makes us unique from other individuals. Identity is destiny.

Destiny is something you discover not fight for. The more we struggle to establish and assert our identity the more it eludes us. However when we let go and just let life flow, serendipity has a way of acknowledging our identity and letting us know.

The quest for meaning and search for significance is an amazing part of the human experience. We determine who we are, our identities, by knowing where we have come from and where we are going. Yet at the same time our past does not necessarily need to define our identity, nor our present behaviors. We can choose to orient ourselves and identify with our future, who we are endeavoring to become.

As you confidently feel what it is like to be the person you aspire to be, you can embrace that identity and then journey toward becoming. In other words you must already inwardly *be* before you can *become*. Destiny is determined by identity.

Looking merely at what we do does not enable us to fully determine who we are. Identity is more than our behavior. Our identity is derived from the decisions we make about ourselves, what we've decided to fuse ourselves with. We become the labels we give ourselves. The way we define our identity defines our life.

There is more to you than meets the eye. People are like onions with layers that need to be peeled so you can get to the core. The labels others give you do not need to minimize and dwarf the totality of who you are. Self-image is not something to work on; it is something to let go of. Once you know who you are, you don't continually need others to affirm you based on your performance, external appearance or their opinion of you.

Once you know who you are, you can do away with the dominant unmet need that drives you to be affirmed for who you truly are. Sadly our culture often seduces us into suppressing who we really are in order to be accepted. In suppressing who we really are we learn how to play the game, push down our feelings, deny our hurts and move meaninglessly through life.

Clothed with our "self-image" wardrobe we pretend everything is wonderful while we're disintegrating inside. Don't project a phony self-image while you are disintegrating within.

You were born an original. Do not therefore die a copy. You cannot copy another person's life. You have to become true to your own identity.

If you feel certain that you are an outstanding person, than you will tap the resources of behavior that match your identity.

An Olympic hopeful diver I know says to herself before she approaches the diving board: "You're a champion! You're the best. You can do it!" She is both affirming her identity and resourcefully accessing her destiny.

Our capability remains constant, but how much of it we use depends upon the identity we give ourselves. Whether you see yourself as a "wimp," a "wild man," a "winner," or a "wallflower," will instantly shape which capabilities you access. If your identity is specifically linked to your age or how you look, you are definitely setting yourself up for future pain as the outward appearance is sure to change. Only when we have a broader sense of who we are is our identity secure and steadfast.

As for me I know myself to be a Dream-Maker, Liberator, Revolutionary, Pioneer, Entrepreneur, Orator, Author, World Traveling Explorer, Missionary Statesman, Prophet and Apostle.

By no means do you have to agree with me. Each individual's reality is essentially determined by their own perception. Personal perception leads to all projection. We will all act consistently with our views of who we truly are, whether that view is accurate or not.

What then is your identity? How would you describe it? Better yet, what do you see about yourself? Can you express it in the form of an image or symbol?

I see myself as a lighthouse illuminating the path for people; a sledgehammer providing needed breakthroughs; a sword cutting through limiting beliefs and a heart providing nurturing acceptance and unconditional love.

Identity is destiny. Therefore the internal imagery that we have about ourselves is vital and worthy of our attention. Likewise it behooves us to know the identity of others (how they see themselves), particularly a potential spouse.

Because each will travel toward the establishing of their identity, which is destiny, it is crucial that we know who we are traveling with. If we have two separate destinations in mind, we might both get lost and never arrive at the intended destination. Two visions lead to division.

Therefore there must be some overlap, or at the very least an understanding of the identities and destinies of each individual prior to marriage. Otherwise you will either journey alone and have nobody to enjoy the experience with or one may find fulfillment while the other sacrifices their own identity.

To assure maximum fulfillment for both persons, a happy pursuit of personal destinies and an enjoyable journey for both partners - understanding each other's identity is extremely important. Upon examining and determining the issue of identity many will quickly realize the incongruent areas in their relationship and want to part ways. Others will suddenly realize why they intuitively clicked and were able to have so much in common all along. From this issue of identity new discoveries will be made as this question of identity welcomes us to explore ourselves from a deeper place far beneath the mental arena.

Symbols can provide us a metaphorical meaning and an analogy, which further illustrates and explains the identity we see internally but cannot quite articulate verbally. Therefore feel free to use symbols and metaphors as needed to express your identity, discover the identity of those closest to you and assess compatibility issues.

This can all seem very esoteric unless we start to actually define ourselves. Take a moment to define who you are. There are so many ways in which we can define ourselves. Who are you?

Allow yourself to drift to an emotional state of curiosity and intrigue where you ask yourself "Who am I?"

Perhaps you have never been called upon to think about such a topic and answer such a probing question. Leave it to me to ask the hard questions. One easy out is to apply the "Popeye Principle" which basically says, "I am what I am, and that's all I am." Yet that won't serve you well nor establish a meaningful identity with which to carry you into your destiny.

Don't fear exploring this issue of identity because as you do clarity will increasingly come as you give yourself liberty to think in this direction. Let whatever answers come steadily flow. Write them down as they do.

Key Points Review

It takes two to know one. You can't know yourself *by* yourself.

We know ourselves in relation to others. Often it is the feedback of others who can see and kindly acknowledge our gifts that both affirm us and enable us to know who we are.

Do not allow yourself to be pigeon-holed by another's limited mindset or miniscule ideological orbit.

Don't embrace labels that dwarf, confine and restrict us from further evolving and growing.

Identity is simply our sense of certainty about who we are. It defines our individuality and creates our world.

We define ourselves not only by who we are, but also by who we are not.

Identity is our most core belief about our personhood, what makes us unique from other individuals.

Identity is destiny. Destiny is something you discover not fight for.

The more we struggle to establish and assert our identity the more it eludes us.

When we let go and just let life flow, serendipity has a way of acknowledging our identity and letting us know.

We determine who we are, our identities, by knowing where we have come from and where we are going. Yet our past does not necessarily need to define our identity, nor our present behaviors. We can choose to orient ourselves and identify with our future, who we are and the person we are endeavoring to become.

As you confidently feel what it is like to be the person you aspire to be, you can embrace that identity and then journey toward becoming. In other words you must already inwardly *be* before you can *become*.

Looking merely at what we do does not enable us to fully determine who we are. Identity is more than our behavior. Our identity is derived from the decisions we make about ourselves, what we've decided to fuse ourselves with.

People are like onions with layers that need to be peeled so you can get to the core. The labels others give you do not need to minimize and dwarf the totality of who you are.

Sadly our culture often seduces us into suppressing who we really are in order to be accepted. In suppressing who we really are we learn how to play the game, push down our feelings, deny our hurts and move meaninglessly through life.

Don't project a phony self-image while you are disintegrating within. Be authentic and true to your own identity.

Only when we have a broader sense of who we are is our identity secure and steadfast.

Each individual's reality is essentially determined by their own perception. Personal perception leads to all projection. We will all act consistently with our views of who we are, whether that view is accurate or not.

Because each will travel toward the establishing of their identity, which is destiny, it is crucial that we know who we are traveling with. If we have two separate destinations in mind, we might both get lost and never arrive at the intended destination. Two visions lead to division.

From this issue of identity new discoveries will be made as this question of identity welcomes us to explore ourselves from a deeper place far beneath the mental arena.

Allow yourself to drift to an emotional state of curiosity and intrigue where you ask yourself "Who am I?"

You never need to be a prisoner to your past nor bound to your behavior.

Your identity evolves essentially from that which you choose to identify with. That being said you can transform and expand your identity, thereby altering your entire life. You can always decide to redefine yourself.

Identity shifts can be exciting, magical and liberating moments.

Like the cartoon character the incredible Hulk you too can breakout and become all you desire to be! First however you must *be* it within and own that identity before you can manifest its reality.

Questions to Ask Yourself and Others

- Who are you?

- Define yourself?

- What is your identity?

- What core belief do you hold about yourself that proves to be an anchor within?

- What images come to mind when you consider your identity?

- Do you have any metaphors to further describe your identity?

- What are you not?

- Describe your experience of the gap between your expectations of reality, and the reality of your expectations?

- How do other people see you?

- In what ways have you at times in your life denied or pulled back from your true authentic self so as to not feel the pain of being left out and to maintain peer approval?

- If you were to look in the dictionary under your name, what would it say?

- If you were to create an ID card that would represent who you truly are, what would be on it and what would you leave off?

- If you were to write your obituary following your death, what would you want it to read?

- If you were given five words to write on your tombstone at death, what would they be?

- What do you want to be remembered for?

Life is marked by seasons of stability as well as crisis. There are seasons when you are really excited about who you are, and other times when you are in crisis concerning your roles. Sometimes you can go through turbulent seasons in your life because who you have been no longer serves to help you become who you desire to be.

Dr. Mark Chironna poignantly points out in his masterpiece *You Can Let Go Now*,

> "How do you know who you really are? You grow up in a world where, from the time you

are little, you are expected to fulfill certain roles. You have to be a child, student, son or daughter, foster child, adoptee, or whatever. You are shaped in part not only by what you feel from a deep place inside, but also by what is directing you from the outside: parental expectations, peer pressure, environment, and culture. Usually you don't pick your boundaries in your formative years; they are picked for you.[1]

It isn't until you leave the nest, get out on your own, and do 'your thing' that you begin to test those boundaries in order to find out what does or doesn't fit in your life, who you are, and, most importantly, who you are not. The truth is that those issues don't come to the surface until we are just about ready to leave home or have left home."

Deep patterns engrained in our being cause us to take "home" (good or bad) with us whether we want to or not. Yet most of us try to disassociate from being a photocopy of Mom and Dad. The irony however is your home environment has taken up residence within you and is sure to manifest itself wherever you go. When it does you must recognize it as having come from where you have been and determine whether or not you want it to be a part of where you are going. You never need to be a prisoner to your past nor bound to your behaviors.

Your identity evolves essentially from that which

---

1. (p.78, You Can Let Go Now, Mark J. Chironna, Nelson Books, 2004)

you choose to identify with. That being said you can transform and expand your identity, thereby altering your entire life. You can always decide to redefine yourself.

Identity shifts can be exciting, magical and liberating moments. I recall during my childhood imagining I was Superman and could fly. Then I would be Batman and tell Robin what to do. Once I discovered baseball I began imitating every batter in the Yankees lineup. I could go down the line and stand in the batter's box and hold my bat just like each of them. From the time I got up in the morning until the time I went to bed, I breathed baseball. My identity and dream was to be a pro-baseball player.

Since that time my identity has further deepened, broadened, expanded and evolved becoming fuller and more fulfilling. Today I am a dream-maker, liberator, entrepreneur, fitness trainer, life coach, world traveling explorer, author, public speaker, TV producer, consultant, minister, son, brother, friend, grandson and so much more!

Like the cartoon character the incredible Hulk, you too can breakout and become all you desire to be! First however you must *be* it within and own that identity before you can manifest its reality. Being means breathing, walking, talking, thinking, feeling and carrying yourself with that knew identity always in full focus before you. As you do, your identity will take you to your destiny.

Consider Core Values

Values guide our every decision and therefore determine our destiny. Leaders are those who know their values, live by them unashamedly and pioneer a path for others to follow. To obtain the highest level of fulfillment in life it is paramount that we first decide upon what we value most in life. We must know what is important to us.

Many when they get what they want, do not want what they've got. Why not? Because they never took time to examine and assess their values. They were chasing red herrings not really knowing what they truly were seeking. Therefore they were without any clear and concise direction by which they can navigate their lives.

Your values provide you a personal compass to chart the course of your life.

If you never stand for something, you will fall for anything. What values do you stand for? The reason people find themselves in tight spots, unable to make tough decisions with clarity is because they are unclear about their personal values. All decision-making comes down to the clarification of your values.

Once you know what is important to you, making key decisions are easy. When you don't know your values you are double minded and therefore unstable in all of your ways. I have been there before. It is inwardly tormenting and not an enjoyable place to be.

Why do so many people hate their jobs? It is because they are working in a profession that is not congruent with their inner core values. Others may have found their desirable profession, but they are among the wrong people who don't hold their values and thus they feel as if they are being violated everyday they go to work.

A fewer number may be in the wrong geographical place where the values they esteem are not a priority. There are obvious differences between the culture of the northeastern United States and the deep southern Bible belt. The foundational values within those places affect the cultural flow and feel of the region.

Values, whether known or unknown, create a magnetic pull of sorts that channel our energy and direct our lives. Those who know their values can set their face like flint and be led by them. Those who do not know their values can be led here, there and everywhere by whoever they allow into their lives.

Values anchor us and provide stability of character. Is it any wonder 60% of all marriages in the United States end in divorce when the people of our great nation are going through an individual identity crisis and have not grasped the importance of knowing their values? If the foundation is not sure how can the marriage be built to last?

America's identity crisis and divorce dilemma should be no surprise when the nation itself over the past few decades has experienced a major shift in its own values thanks to the media and the Supreme Court's reinterpretation of the Constitution.

By no means have the values of the Founding Fathers of the United States been upheld. Two-thirds of the signers of the Declaration of Independence were graduates from Biblical seminaries. They were men who valued godliness, purity, integrity, fidelity and honor. Today the ACLU has boldly assaulted the very values the Founding Fathers upheld, endeavoring to remove every mention of God from our public institutions. It is no coincidence that the 10 Commandments were historically displayed in many of our states' supreme courthouses. Atheism was not a value of the Founding Fathers of America.

If we are to experience liberty and justice for all as the Founding Fathers intended, we would do well to again uphold and esteem their values that birthed our great nation. The Liberty Bell at Independence Hall in Philadelphia quotes a Scripture from the Bible in the book of Leviticus concerning liberty. Our country's core foundational values were Biblically based and don't let anyone else tell you otherwise.

Long-term happiness and fulfillment can only be assured when you commit to live by and not deviate from your values. Get clear about what is most important in your life and decide to hold true to your values regardless of situational circumstances. With or without the support of those you love and esteem, you make the choice to hold to and be guided by your inner values.

Your personal values are more valuable than things. What good are things if you have to violate your self-worth to get them? *Being* by far surpasses *having*. Possessing things will never satisfy your soul nor make you whole as a person. Your life does not consist in the abundance of things that you possess. The sense of certainty and "straight as an arrow" focus you will get from discovering and holding to your values is priceless. Upon integrating the parts of your life in accordance with your values you will find your center and become unshakeable in all things.

Living by your values will make life incredibly rich and intoxicating for you. When you live by your values, eliminating all other distractions that don't satisfy becomes easy. The momentary "quick fixes" that we fill our lives with temporarily to make us feel better when we are on a downward spiral all lose their pull on us once we come into alignment with our values.

Relational intimacy and meeting your deepest emotional needs requires an understanding of values. You're not likely to hit a target when you are blindfolded and don't know where it is.

We experientially (often unbeknownst to ourselves) set up our values based on lifelong conditioning as we have encountered pleasure and pain. Punishment and reward are huge motivators, which determine what you desire to move toward and also away from.

Heroes and villains also possess values we model depending upon the extent of their influence upon us. Many of our youth have gone "ghetto" today. Kids from the suburbs dress, talk and walk like the boys in the hood. Bad boys are on the rise as the youth culture is gravitating toward them, their rebellion and uninhibited expression of their sexuality.

Churches are the pillars of truth in our nation, which emphasize values we can use both in and out of the home. Unless churches modernize their message and connect with the culture, another generation will be lost because of religion's inability to relate.

Due to the decline of public education, schools cannot be depended upon to instill values within our children anymore. This explains why private schools are increasing and becoming more popular across the country. Parents are waking up to the woes of the public school system and its outdated modes of education.

It is the job of parents to impart their values and philosophy to their children. Sadly most children are being babysat by the TV, "the one-eyed demon" as one preacher called it. When the average person watches seven hours of TV a day, is it any wonder our nation is experiencing such a moral decline, a drop in test scores and the disintegration of the traditional family structure?

When assessing your values it is important to differentiate between means and ends. If I were to ask you, "What do you value most?" you might answer, "Love, money, sex ...." Of these, love is the *ends* value you are seeking; the emotion you desire. Money and sex might merely be a *means* that you believe will get you the recognition and love you really want.

So to cut to the chase, ask yourself "What does that do for you?" In other words if I said, "What does success do for you?" You might reply, "Success causes me to feel fulfilled and be financially secure." What you truly value therefore (the *ends* you are after) is fulfillment and security.

Money means different things to different people. For some it may mean freedom, whereas to others it may embody the ability to help humanity in the form of contribution. Repeatedly ask yourself, "What does that do for you?" and follow your responses to the deeper set of values and emotions you truly long to experience.

Your values are your motivators, "hot buttons," neurological stimulators and the source of emotional octane to propel you forward. Explore now and list your hierarchy of values, the emotional states you most deeply desire.

To help you along, here is a list of some positive moving toward values you can choose from (and happily add to as it by no means is exhaustive). Put them in the order of importance for you, number 1 being the highest.

Moving-Toward Values

Freedom
Contribution
Accomplishment
Fulfillment
Opportunity
Security
Peace
Personal Growth
Intellectual Stimulation
Happiness
Creativity
Fun
Resourcefulness
Love
Success
Intimacy
Adventure
Power
Passion
Comfort
Health

For me the values of love, intimacy, passion, health, freedom, adventure, creativity, contribution, personal growth and fulfillment are of utmost importance. I believe as I experience these values success and accomplishment will automatically come. What values most influence you? It is perfectly all right to be given to change your values at times as you evolve and reprioritize your life. Be careful however not to violate your values because of pressing needs. Many violate their values to meet their needs and in the end find themselves unhappy.

> For me I highly value:
> 1. Love
> 2. Health
> 3. Laughter and Childlike Playfulness
> 4. Self-Expression
> 5. Adventure
> 6. Spirituality
> 7. Creativity
> 8. Contribution
> 9. Prosperity
> 10. Legacy

The forces of pain and pleasure can positively influence your life if you can discover how you are emotionally wired, honestly acknowledge your neurological tendencies and master your moods. We previously looked at moving toward values. Now let's examine some moving away from values.

Every decision we are called upon to make immediately is processed through the brain in such a way to evaluate both the inherent possible pleasure and pain. Your brain amazingly knows (based upon your values - whether you consciously know them or not) how to weigh, evaluate and filter through the various alternatives, while also simultaneously assessing the corresponding impact of each possible decision.

The relative levels of pain we associate with various emotions will heavily affect all of our decisions.

As it pertains to avoidance, what emotions do you most often tend to resist experiencing? Again numerically list them in order of importance, the emotion you most dislike and most want to avoid being number one.

Moving-Away From Values

Fear
Anger
Guilt
Humiliation
Isolation
Loneliness
Depression
Rejection
Confusion
Failure
Frustration
Helplessness

For me I gravitate and earnestly move away from depression, rejection, loneliness and fear by aggressively moving forth into my future, reiterating my identity and doing things that immediately fulfill and make me happy. If I ever feel a bit down (which is rare) I begin to dance to music, go to the gym where I can be in a lively atmosphere where people are moving, or surf some waves to get an adrenalin rush.

Moving toward and moving away from values determine your behavior in any given environment. Most people however do more to avoid pain than they will do to gain pleasure. The majority of us will do whatever is necessary, consciously or unconsciously, to keep from experiencing pain.

If you beat a dog long enough, the next time he sees you he will run. We are no different emotionally as we get closer to situations that could produce possible pain for us. The problem is often those same situations can also procure sizeable gains and pleasure as well. Which value then should we listen to - the moving toward or moving away from value? I say the moving toward value!

All of us have some degree of values conflicts within because we are human and thus shy away from any infliction of pain upon ourselves. This however is where we must be willing to be vulnerable and take risks, considering the gains and pleasure of greater values than the possible temporary pain. If you don't take chances you don't make advances.

As it pertains to assessing a future spouse, if adventure is high up on your list of values and security is top priority for her - you might not be a good match. You want to look for someone with similar values or at least workable values that blend and flow with your own. Otherwise your relationship will continually collide as each of you pursue different values and remain continually at odds with each other in doing so.

Key Points Review

Values guide our every decision and therefore determine our destiny.

To obtain the highest level of fulfillment in life it is paramount that we first decide upon what we value most in life.

Many when they get what they want, do not want what they've got. Why not? Because they never took time to examine and assess their values.

Your values provide you a personal compass to chart the course of your life.

If you never stand for something, you will fall for anything.

All decision-making comes down to the clarification of your values.

Values anchor us and provide stability of character.

Atheism was not a value of the Founding Fathers of America.

Possessing things will never satisfy your soul nor make you whole as a person.

Living by your values will make life incredibly rich and intoxicating for you.

Relational intimacy and meeting your deepest emotional needs requires an understanding of values.

Due to the decline of public education, schools cannot be depended upon to instill values within our children anymore.

When assessing your values it is important to differentiate between means and ends.

Your values are your motivators, "hot buttons," neurological stimulators and the source of emotional octane to propel you forward.

Many violate their values to meet their needs and in the end find themselves unhappy.

The forces of pain and pleasure can positively influence your life if you can discover how you are emotionally wired, honestly acknowledge your neurological tendencies and master your moods.

Questions to Ask Yourself and Others

1. What are your motivators?
2. What aspirations do you have for yourself and the future?
3. What do you value most in your friends?
4. What do you value most in yourself?
5. Who are your heroes? Why?
6. What things irritate you the most about people?

7. What personality traits do you despise and resist at all costs?
8. What values do you most desire in a future spouse? Some examples:
    - "I most value purity, honesty and integrity."
    - "Gentleness, affectionate and tenderness are my top priority."
    - "Wisdom, restraint and quietness are of most value for me when considering a spouse."
9. What are your biggest fears?
10. What emotions do you least like having to feel?
11. What emotions do you enjoy experiencing the most?
12. What are your top de-motivators eliciting emotions you find least desirable?
13. Considering your new understanding of your motivators and de-motivators, what type of spouse would be best for you?
14. What type of spouse, speaking of internal values and personality, would be least suitable for you?

Identify Beliefs

Beliefs guide us to conclusions teaching us how to feel and what to do. There are different levels of beliefs that have different levels of impact on the quality of our lives. *Global beliefs* have an all-encompassing expansive influence on our life. These global beliefs have much further reaching consequences.

Global beliefs concern what you believe about people (gender, races, ages), yourself, opportunity, time, scarcity and abundance. It is vital that we examine our beliefs and their respective consequences to make sure they are empowering us. Many what I call "assumicide" by never questioning their beliefs nor the outcomes (or lack thereof) they are getting from adhering to them.

I'm reminded of the movie *Remember the Titans* when "the running back" smiling from ear to ear met his new coach. The coach asked: "Why are you smiling?" The young man replied, "Because football is fun." When the coach challenged that belief, he suddenly stopped smiling and came to know the coach's point of reference - that football is work, hard work.

Neither belief was right nor wrong, but upon meeting each other there was a full on perceptual collision. Our lives often are no different when circumstances come into play and provide us opportunity to further test and evaluate our underlying beliefs.

The beliefs you have about people in general (good or bad) will affect not just the way you deal with a family member or close friend, but with all people you meet. Such beliefs positively or negatively impact your ability to trust, the quality of your relationships, your effectiveness in your career, the success of your marriage and much more.

Because I experienced numerous challenges with women growing up, I had some underlying subconscious beliefs about women that surfaced when I got married. My grandmother was a bit grumpy. My mother was an alcoholic and drug addict. My stepmom and I had some challenges when I moved in to live with my dad and her. Therefore I did not know how to properly relate to women. I never had a sister either, which left me a bit clueless as to the opposite sex. I had a tainted point of reference. It took time for me to overcome my distrust of women and to realize not all women are a pain in the butt. In fact I discovered that women keep the world a civilized place by often keeping men in check. It is women that enable us to feel and live from the heart.

Another limiting belief concerns scarcity. If you believe there is not enough in this world to go around it will cause you to be competitive in your nature and view people who potentially could assist you in your life's purpose as enemies rather than friends. Thus you would repel the very people your purpose requires you to attract. Erroneous beliefs cause you to repel the people your life's purpose requires you to attract.

Many people in our country grew up with a parent who was abusive or a substance abuser. This they may say is the reason they are not successful today. Nothing is farther from the truth. I myself had a drug addict and alcoholic for a mother. I could have easily played the victim. Instead I chose to be the victor and turn the mess into a message whereby I could feed and strengthen multitudes. You see it is not the events of our lives that shape us, but rather our beliefs as to what those events mean.

I myself have learned to consider every obstacle a stepping stone; every pain a platform to powerfully communicate from; every hurt healing for the masses; every mess a dynamic message in the making and today's test tomorrow's testimony. When life gives you a lemon, make some lemonade.

When you bake a cake there are many ingredients that all alone by themselves would not taste so great. Yet when you put it all together and throw it in the oven, a delicious masterpiece comes forth. Take all your life's experiences and put them together in such a way that serves you.

Another example of a global belief could be: "All men care about is sex." I don't underestimate the critical circumstances in which such beliefs are formed. Perhaps you were raped by somebody or molested by a trusted family member. We all can empathize with such hardships. For those of you who have been bruised and broken by such traumatic experiences, please read my book *Breakthrough for a Broken Heart*. You can overcome your disappointments and blossom into your dreams.

Sexist limiting beliefs skew your ability to relate to the entire gender, which is half the planet. Having sexist beliefs about men will cause you to see men in a way that cuts you off from all the other blessings that having a male family member, co-worker, friend or spouse can provide for you.

Some limiting beliefs about success that could be sabotaging you are:

"I'm black and there are no opportunities for us to get ahead."

"If you are going to get ahead you have to work hard."

"There never is enough time."

"My English isn't good enough to get the kind of job I want."

"If you don't get a good government job, then you will never be able to retire and have anything when you are old."

Another set of limiting beliefs can be how we relate to our Creator. As a life coach, I had the privilege of working with a dynamic woman within the health & nutrition industry. As we explored her identity and the way she saw herself, some limiting beliefs arose concerning her Creator.

Basically she saw herself as unworthy and was living in a state of condemnation. Once the heart of the Creator (with all His unconditional love, acceptance and forgiveness) was made known and felt, deliverance from this limiting belief occurred.

Some limiting beliefs about God can be:

"God is all about me serving Him and doesn't care about my personal happiness."

"God doesn't want women to work outside the home."

"God created women to serve men."

"Women must submit to their husbands in all situations."

Sadly religion often oppresses women more than anybody else. Most religious texts were written by men (regardless of their source of inspiration – often not God). Therefore when they are interpreted by modern-day priests, typically and predominately men, is it any wonder they are most often used to serve men while enslaving women? The heart of the Creator however is for the freedom and self-determination of all people - male or female.

All of these disempowering beliefs must be eliminated from your thinking. As you think, so shall you be (Proverbs 23:7). Your perception is ultimately your projection. Jesus said, "According to your faith, be it unto you" (Matthew 9:29).

Don't set yourself up for continual failure and heartache by incorrectly programming your computer - the brain that sits atop your shoulders. Begin to brainstorm all the beliefs you have (big and small) that empower and disempower you.

All personal breakthroughs begin with a change in beliefs. Things do not change; we change.

Key Points Review

Beliefs guide us to conclusions teaching us how to feel and what to do.

Global beliefs have an all-encompassing expansive influence on our life.

It is vital that we examine our beliefs and their respective consequences to make sure they are empowering us.

Beliefs positively or negatively impact your ability to trust, the quality of your relationships, your effectiveness in your career, the success of your marriage and much more.

Erroneous beliefs cause you to repel the people your life's purpose requires you to attract.

It is not the events of our lives that shape us, but rather our beliefs as to what those events mean.

Take all your life's experiences and put them together in such a way that serves you.

The heart of the Creator however is for the freedom and self-determination of all people - male or female.

Your perception is ultimately your projection.

Don't set yourself up for continual failure and heartache by incorrectly programming your computer - the brain that sits atop your shoulders.

Begin to brainstorm all the beliefs you have (big and small) that empower and disempower you.

All personal breakthroughs begin with a change in beliefs. Things do not change; we change.

During the course of your interaction and relationship with people note broad generalizations that are made in conversation. Note compartmentalizing, wide-sweeping generalities in words like *never* and *always*.

Disempowering beliefs can continually cause conflict relationally, professionally and personally. Unfinished business may not be ideal to marry into but should rather first be dealt with prior to making a matrimonially covenant for life.

Values and beliefs are essentially the governing internal laws by which we live and move in society. Their importance cannot be evaluated and emphasized enough, particularly when assessing relational compatibility.

Notice knee jerk reactions in certain social settings and when specific topics of discussion come up.

Observing nonverbal behavior and actively listening will enable you to get a glimpse of underlying beliefs that a person may not have yet revealed about themselves.

Listening to people's vocabulary is an excellent way to assess their beliefs.

The mouth reveals what the heart believes. From the overflow of the heart come the words of the mouth. As a man believes, so does he speak.

Questions to Ask Yourself and Others

- What are your global beliefs?

- How are your beliefs empowering or disempowering you?

- Do you believe people are good or bad?

- Do you believe people are trustworthy or not?

Are You Ready For True Love?

- What do you believe about men?
- What do you believe about women?
- Are there any people that you dislike? Why?
- Complete the sentence: Men must _____
- Complete the sentence: Men should _____
- Complete the sentence: Men never _____
- Complete the sentence: Men always _____
- Complete the sentence: Women must _____
- Complete the sentence: Women should _____
- Complete the sentence: Women never _____
- Complete the sentence: Women always _____
- What do you believe about yourself?
- Do you believe you are a giver or inclined to be a taker?
- Are you generous or selfish?
- Are you happy or moody?
- Are you intelligent or mentally challenged?

- Are you beautiful, average or ugly?

- Are you sexy or less desirable?

- Are you adventurous or more calculating, preferring to play it safe?

- Are you a lover or a fighter?

- Do you take things at face value or question them?

- Are you a spender or a saver?

- Do you prepare for opportunities or crises?

- Are you passionate or complacent?

- Do you relate well to people or get uncomfortable in the presence of people?

- Do you believe time is plenteous or not enough?

- Do you use time wisely giving thought to its allocation or freely without thought?

- Do you feel pressed for time or at leisure to enjoy time?

- Do you believe you must make time or take time?

- Do you believe there is only so much to go around or a never-ending supply of resources?

Are You Ready For True Love?

- Do you have an inner tendency toward wealth & abundance or a predisposition toward lack and poverty?

- What do you believe about abundance and wealth?

- What do you believe about resources?

- What do you believe about the "Haves" and "Have-nots"?

- Do you believe women are to work outside the home or stay at home to care for the children and house?

- Do you believe children should care for their elderly parents or that a nursing home with assisted living is an option?

- At what age do you believe children can make their own decisions?

- At what age are children no longer obliged to answer to their parents?

- What do you believe is the best way to deal with conflict?

- What are your strategies for conflict resolution?

- How do you manage your emotions when under stress?

- What do you expect of others close to you when you are going through a crisis?

- What do you believe is necessary for you to be liked and to feel good about yourself?

During the course of your interaction and relationship with people note broad generalizations that are made in conversation. Such as, "Men *never* care what women want. They *always* just want one thing."

Note compartmentalizing, wide-sweeping generalities in words like *never* and *always*. These words enable you to pick up on underlying beliefs at the core of the person's psyche. Such beliefs guide the framework of our lives and the way we situationally relate to people.

Such remarks, statements and comments should be red flags to note as these bold and blatant statements tending toward generalization can be crippling on the long term when brought face to face with situations that collide head on with such beliefs. Disempowering beliefs of this sort can continually cause conflict relationally, professionally and personally. Unfinished business of this sort may not be ideal to marry into but should rather first be dealt with prior to making a matrimonially covenant for life.

Values and beliefs are essentially the governing internal laws by which we live and move in society. Their importance cannot be evaluated and emphasized enough, particularly when assessing relational compatibility.

Are You Ready For True Love?

Notice knee jerk reactions in certain social settings and when specific topics of discussion come up. One young lady whom I was considering marrying, firmly believed I did not trust her. She felt I did not trust her simply because I disagreed with her on the handling of an issue regarding real estate.

By no means is one disagreement sufficient ground to not trust someone. Yet in her mind, the belief was substantiated by a single disagreement. Can you imagine what kind of marriage we would have had with this mindset? Disagreements and conflicts, which must be worked through, abound in marriage. If any mild disagreement is reason to distrust, than you had better reconsider getting involved with such a fragile person.

These are the kind of knee jerk reactions I'm talking about. Often you will not discover them until you are close enough to a person to watch and observe them on a daily basis and hear their manner of communication. Observing nonverbal behavior and actively listening will enable you to get a glimpse of underlying beliefs that a person may not have yet revealed about themselves.

For example, one young lady I dated, upon looking at some shirts in my closet, told me: "Those are playboy shirts." To me however they were nothing of the sort. They were elegant and stylish shirts with colors and a few buttons. There weren't any bunnies on them. None of my friends had ever commented about my clothes or warned me about being a playboy. To this lady however (perhaps because they weren't bland work shirts) they symbolized the dress of a playboy (a judgment she was making of me based on her belief of people's clothing).

Yet if we were to dig deeper (which I will), we would find past unfaithfulness in this lady's previous relationships. Therefore her great value of loyalty led her to boldly move away from anything that looked like unfaithfulness based on her previous experiences. Apparently she anchored certain clothes to infidelity and her knee-jerk reaction was to immediately become accusatory upon seeing any shirts of mine that resembled the same style of her previous unfaithful boyfriend.

By the way, nobody else has ever made any negative comments about those shirts and I have worn them many times even to church on occasion. Such knee-jerk reactions and commentary is what you want to keep your eyes and ears open to when considering someone for marriage.

Vocabulary

Listening to people's vocabulary is an excellent way to assess their beliefs. It does not take long to quickly get a grasp of what someone believes. Just hang around them long enough and listen to them talk. The mouth reveals what the heart believes. From the overflow of the heart come the words of the mouth. As a man believes, so does he speak.

Therefore if you hear something that someone says and it agitates your spirit within, that is a red flag that an illogical or destructive belief is in operation.

Birds of a feather flock together. Show me your friends and I will show you your future. Be selective therefore who you hang with.

Assess Mental Models & Mindsets

Beyond beliefs we must evaluate the way people use their computer on top of their shoulders. Some I might add have a better working computer than others. Mental models and mindsets greatly vary among people. Allow me to explain.

One personal pet peeve of mine has always been the tendency to jump to illogical conclusions. For example if I am with a woman and I see another lady walk by in a lovely dress, I might say "Wow! I really like that dress." An illogical response from the woman I'm with would be, "What, you don't like my clothes?"

These type of "if" this "then" that illogical remarks are aggravating, not to mention personally destructive to the person making them. Such a line of reasoning would say that if I like a beautiful house in the new subdivision, I dislike my own home where I live. Certainly however this is not the case.

The way we mentally and cognitively process information and outside stimuli is very important, as it will determine our actions and reactions. An erroneous perception can lead to an inappropriate projection.

One the other side of the coin, it has been said that women have a good intuition. That is to say they are feelers and can sense things that often men overlook. Intuition is like a seventh sense. Women it seems are more alert as it pertains to the totality of the senses and therefore are more "in-to-it" as it applies to the moment. Being fully present requires you to harness your spirit, mind and body simultaneously to be alert.

Intuition requires we be fully present with the moment, mentally alert and not wandering away somewhere in our mind.

So if I were to put together a checklist for assessing one's mental and cognitive faculties it might read like this.

1. Are they college educated?
2. Do they have any particular skill?
3. What are their gifts and talents?
4. How good is their intuition?
5. What mental strategies do they employ under pressure? For example when you are running late and you can't find your keys? When you are dealing with resolving family conflict? When your credit card has unauthorized charges on it? When you are overseas and having to deal with cross-cultural challenges with which you have no previous experience?
6. How do they solve problems? What methods and strategies do they employ both externally and internally as it pertains to managing their emotions? Do they lose it and explode

verbally? Can they effectively govern themselves and situations that came upon them unexpectedly?
7. How do they seek to exert their influence? For example when they want something? Do they become manipulative, resort to flattery, verbally explode or simply express their desire? When they are in a disagreement do they attack the other person verbally, physically get violent, or peaceably seek mutual understanding? If they feel threatened due to insecurity or jealousy, do they resort to slander and verbal abuse of the other individual? Are they humble and self-aware, willing to acknowledge their struggles and fears?

The list of possible scenarios are endless. However these heated moments are wonderful opportunities to see a person in action and observe how they deal with and mentally move through situations. Everyone's approach, perception, processing and problem solving methods differ. You therefore must get a sense for the person's demeanor, mannerism and mental model. As you do it will enable you to see if you gel and are a good fit, or if there are some discrepancies and potentially trouble spots to work on if you are to stay together.

8. What assumptions do they tend toward relationally and professionally?

Assumptions are a deadly thing in that they commit you to a path and course of action often prematurely before adequately gathering all necessary information to make a fully informed decision. The fact of the matter is our intuition is often wrong. People often mentally work out of generalizations, deletions and distortions. This enables us to process information and more quickly size up a situation. The problem is our assessment of people and situations is often at first sight wrong. As it is said, "You cannot judge the book by the cover."

People who jump to conclusions and make hasty judgments are those who make many assumptions. Before making a life commitment to someone, you would do well to assess the assumptions they make, live by and project on others. Assumptions lead to "assumicide" and that is not a pleasant experience.

9. To what extent do outside forces affect their mental model and cognitive processing?

When I speak of outside forces, I am referring to parental patterning and also the spiritual realm. We often duplicate our parents' mental model and communication style unless we sincerely saw its flaws and frailties for what they were and objectively decided against it (even if only in part).

A discerning heart and mind will honestly look at the good and bad of parental projection as it pertains to mental models we may have learned and their convictions we may have caught (be they right or wrong).

Another outside force can be the spirit realm. Spiritually minded people are open to insight from their Creator, His Spirit and angelic visitations. If you are an atheist you might not appreciate this too much in a spouse, particularly when they want to tithe their monthly income to the church. Just something to consider before you embrace a person for life. If their mental model does not align or agree with yours you may be in for a bumpy ride.

Key Points Review

The way we mentally and cognitively process information and outside stimuli is very important, as it will determine our actions and reactions.

An erroneous perception can lead to an inappropriate projection.

Intuition is like a seventh sense.

Intuition requires we be fully present with the moment, mentally alert and not wandering away somewhere in our mind.

Heated moments are wonderful opportunities to see a person in action and observe how they deal with and mentally move through situations.

Everyone's approach, perception, processing and problem solving methods differ. You therefore must get a sense for the person's demeanor, mannerism and mental model.

Look for discrepancies and potentially trouble spots to work on if you are to stay together.

Assumptions are a deadly thing in that they commit you to a path and course of action often prematurely before adequately gathering all necessary information to make a fully informed decision.

Our intuition is often wrong. Our assessment of people and situations is often at first sight wrong. You cannot judge the book by the cover.

People who jump to conclusions and make hasty judgments are those who make many assumptions. Before making a life commitment to someone, you would do well to assess the assumptions they make, live by and project on others. Assumptions lead to "assumicide" and that is not a pleasant experience.

We often duplicate our parents' mental model and communication style unless we sincerely see its flaws and frailties for what they are and objectively decide against it (even if only in part).

A discerning heart and mind will honestly look at the good and bad of parental projection as it pertains to mental models we may have learned and their convictions we may have caught (be they right or wrong).

If a person's mental model does not align or agree with yours you may be in for a bumpy ride.

Examine Behavior

The way we believe determines how we behave. As we develop new beliefs about who we are, our behavior will change to support our new identity. Sadly however many people remain rigid, frigid and never update the resume. Therefore we must be discerning enough to note their speech and behavioral patterns to discover the direction of their life. Destiny is determined each and every hour of the day by the things we do and say. Upon making that discovery, it should be quite clear whether or not you'd like to join them in their life's journey based on the direction they are going.

It has been said repeatedly that talk is cheap, as actions speak louder than words. I however want to encourage you to monitor and examine both in a person because each are very revealing. The way your feet move reveals what your heart believes and values.

Beyond merely focusing on the negatives and relational red flags I also want to accentuate the positive. After all you have made it this far and if you are still considering the person you had in mind at the beginning of this book, then it is only right to acknowledge some of the good in them that attracted you in the first place.

What activities do you and your special someone participate in regularly? Do you play any particular sports that are of mutual interest to you? Perhaps you have some similar hobbies or things you like to do together.

I enjoy weight lifting regularly at the health club, surfing when I can get to the beach, playing tennis when I can find a partner, traveling the world, professional speaking and writing. The last of those, professional speaking, is typically something most people fear and dread. It is perfectly fine if my wife does not enjoy communicating in front of large audiences. By no means is that a deal breaker or requirement for me. I just want a beautiful woman inside and out who is crazy about me and supportive in all I do. Happily accompanying me around the world and enjoying the experience is sufficient for me. Yet I would like a degree of understanding and emotional support from her in regard to my career.

This is when body language, nonverbal communication, is most revealing as it shows forth the true heart. The deeper emotions within are not easily hidden and often appear in nonverbal body language. If I need someone congruent with me in my life's purpose and fully supportive by my side, I had better evaluate such a person beforehand in similar situations I anticipate them experiencing with me after marriage. For this reason I always try to see a person overseas, out of their comfort zone, in a cross-cultural context. Much of my life has been spent traveling abroad, so this is a big part of my life.

I took Karla to Holland, France, and Monaco with me before I asked her to marry me. This provided me a glimpse into her resourceful nature and showed me how capable she is at handling change and variables beyond her control. We're happily married today, which is to say she passed the test. Since being married she has also traveled to Australia and Fiji with me. While in Fiji she got to walk through the mud while we were ministering in a small village. She never once complained and she was a great blessing to all.

Your Word & Walk Determines Your Worth

Does the person keep their word or are they quick to make excuses and justify sudden unexpected changes? A person's word and walk is essentially their worth.

Are they punctual or always late? Punctuality is the virtue of princes. I don't know about you, but I do not want to be late everywhere I go throughout my life. Most do not consider such things before marrying a person, but you had better consider such things as it will effect your quality of life.

How does this person treat little people? How does he interact with the convenient store clerk when he is in a hurry? How does she speak to the server at the restaurant? What is his manner of speech and respect toward his mother? The way a man treats and esteems his mother is a good indication of how he will honor you after marriage when familiarity sets in.

Familiarity breeds contempt. Respect is something you must discipline yourself to show others and maintain in your relationships. It is easy to take people for granted when you become overly familiar with them.

The devil is in the details. Be careful to evaluate every behavior and the fruit of their life up until now. Fruit or the lack thereof does not lie.

We need to ask God to help us maintain our high regard for the special people He has brought into our lives and continually honor them so as to preserve and uphold those most prized and cherished relationships.

Is the person you are considering for marriage positive or negative in their attitude and communication? That will determine the temperament and atmosphere you will be inhabiting and coexisting with. Make sure the person is more prone to complement than to ridicule you.

Is the person helpful or hindering? Do they take care of their possessions, strive to maintain their car and home with excellence or is everything falling apart around them? How do they care for their own physical body?

If a person cannot care for their own body, how do you expect them to adequately care for you body and well-being? Is health and nutrition important to them or do they eat like an elementary school kid?

What are their notable strengths and weaknesses? Do they humbly acknowledge and admit their weaknesses, confess their mistakes and strive to improve themselves personally?

Are they more organized or creative? Such information is helpful in order for you to know what tasks to assign to each other to ensure an ongoing and successfully functioning marriage.

What is their communication style? Are they quiet, boisterous, mild, moderate or an introvert? How do they handle conflict resolution? Do they easily make peace and reconcile or do they put up walls and play self-righteous?

Are they easily offended? Do they take days to forgive and move on from emotional hurts and wounds? If so you may want to have them get counseling before marriage to deal with such issues.

Do they receive instruction and correction well? Does the feedback of others mean anything to them or are they only self-absorbed? Do they have a tender and teachable spirit or are they a 'know it all' who listens to nobody?

How well do they handle money? Do they have a savings account? Is their checkbook balanced? What debts do they owe? What is their credit rating? Can they get a loan or is their name no good at the bank? Be careful ladies, once you say 'I do' you get their last name tagged on to your first.

Money matters. Romance without finance is foolishness. You can minimize relational conflict by managing your money well. Things get tight when the money is not right. People get mean when there is not any green!

Do they take responsibility for their mistakes, errors and failures? If not, what escape and cover-up mechanism do they employ? Do they play "the blame game?" Do they point the finger and act like it is your fault to deflect criticism away from them?

Are they suspicious and accusatory? Relationships quickly rust without the foundation of honesty and trust. What level of trust exists in their family that they grew up in? Was their trust violated during their childhood or in previous relationships? If so, the issue of trust must be addressed, stressed and fortified to assure and settle their hearts.

What daily disciplines do they adhere to and follow? Do they have any rituals they practice daily? Do they read the Bible, the morning newspaper, meditate, exercise, partake in a pleasurable hobby or participate in some other activity daily for personal enjoyment and tranquility?

Are they morning or evening oriented? Do they have more energy when they get up or before they go to bed? Sex drives also come into play here accordingly and must be understood.

What actions are they committed to for improving themselves and their lives? If they struggle in a particular area, are they pursuing counseling, reading books about it, associating with men who can help mentor them or have they joined a support group for emotional encouragement? Have they committed to a life of personal growth and if so, what specifically are they now doing?

In a day and age when adultery is glorified and divorce minimized, what commitments will you make to continually fortify your marriage? For example, will you go to a marriage class at church? Will you double-date with other married couples?

For those of you who are still unsure about the person in question and simply need to take it slow while you further assess the situation, consider getting a background check. It would be well worth the investment. You can always get more money, but the time you spend is gone forever. Why waste your time on somebody you are unsure of? If a background check would make you feel better, go ahead and get one.

You may even want to ask the person if you may do so. Some may feel you do not trust them and therefore distance themselves from you. However if they have nothing to hide and deeply love you, they should be able to endure a background check to give you further peace of mind and strengthen the bond of trust.

What is the person's track record in the past concerning previous commitments? Did they follow through unto completion? Or did they get distracted, redirect their affection and never complete what they initially started out to do? Such inability to complete what is started is a warning flag to you that this person may not be capable of keeping their commitments.

I cannot tell you how many times I have heard someone say they will learn how to play the guitar, only to later give up and stop practicing within a couple months. The list of incompletions is endless.

Did the person you are considering spending the rest of your life with finish college? Or did they get sidetracked partying and flunk out? What have they successfully finished in their life? Finishing tasks and things started shows stickability and endurance. Marriage is not a sprint but an endurance run.

Find somebody you can trust who can remain loyal and endure hard times. Character is crucial when you are in the crucible of life enduring undesirable circumstances you did not foresee from the beginning.

Recognize Key Qualities

One behavior I failed to recognize about my ex-wife before marrying her was her assertiveness. This quality can be both good and bad depending upon the context. Following my divorce, while having a good conversation with a friend who was among my groomsmen, he noted an incident I had not been aware of and completely overlooked at the time.

It occurred before the wedding when I was picking out a tuxedo for the wedding. My ex-wife was there and upon seeing the tuxedo I liked promptly spoke up before all the men and said to me: "No, you're not getting that one!" This discerning friend said nothing, but some six years later he told me, "When she said that to you in that manner in front of your friends, I knew you guys were going to have problems."

He was the only one who was super sensitive and discerning enough to see this as a potential problem. Yet he never offered me any advice concerning that incident. I wish he would have. Knowing what I now know, this was a blatant sign of disrespect early on. Proper respect for one another is crucial to sustain a love that lasts a lifetime.

Such intuitive flashes are signals to pay attention, further evaluate, consider more carefully and explore options. Do not disregard behavioral cues that may alert you to potential problems before marriage.

It has been said that "Love is blind." Maybe this is so. Before marriage however we should keep both eyes open. After marriage keeping one eye shut and being gracious to overlook flaws is a good idea.

Life is not the way it is supposed to be. It is the way it is. The way you cope with it makes the difference.

How do you spell relief? When confronted with an unforeseeable fury of festering circumstances, what will you do at the end of the day to stay happy and keep your sanity? Learning how to properly cope with problems is extremely important to ensure your personal well-being and a happy ongoing marriage.

Keep things in perspective and remember to value people over possessions. Problems continually come in all shapes in sizes. Learn how to laughingly live with them and love the precious people around you despite the daily irritants.

Don't expect to change someone after marriage. It simply does not happen. You can't teach an old dog new tricks - at least not easily. Find a dog that suits your fancy and until you do keep looking. What you tolerate will eventually dominate. However you can have more in life if you don't settle for less.

Key Points Review

The way we believe determines how we behave. As we develop new beliefs about who we are, our behavior will change to support our new identity.

Notice speech and behavioral patterns to discover the direction of a person's life. Destiny is determined each and every hour of the day by the things we do and say.

A person's word and walk determines their worth.

How does this person treat little people?

The way a man treats and esteems his mother is a good indication of how he will honor you after marriage when familiarity sets in.

Familiarity breeds contempt. Respect is something you must discipline yourself to show others and maintain in your relationships. It is easy to take people for granted when you become overly familiar with them.

The devil is in the details. Be careful to evaluate every behavior and the fruit of their life up until now. Fruit or the lack thereof does not lie.

Be careful ladies, once you say "I do" you get their last name tagged on to your first.

Money matters. Romance without finance is foolishness. You can minimize relational conflict by managing your money well. Things get tight when the money is not right. People get mean when there is not any green!

Do they take responsibility for their mistakes, errors and failures? If not, what escape and cover-up mechanism do they employ? Do they play "the blame game?" Do they point the finger and act like it is your fault to deflect criticism away from them?

Relationships quickly rust without the foundation of honesty and trust. The issue of trust must be addressed, stressed and fortified to assure and settle their hearts.

What daily disciplines do they adhere to and follow? What are their hobbies and activities that you can find mutual satisfaction participating in?

Have they committed to a life of personal growth and if so, what specifically are they now doing?

What commitments will you make to continually fortify your marriage and guard against adultery?

You can always get more money, but the time you spend is gone forever. Why waste your time on somebody you are unsure of? If a background check would make you feel better, go ahead and get one.

Finishing tasks and things started shows stickability and endurance. Marriage is not a sprint but an endurance run.

Find somebody you can trust who can remain loyal and endure hard times. Character is crucial when you are in the crucible of life enduring undesirable circumstances you did not foresee.

Proper respect for one another is crucial to sustain a love that lasts a lifetime.

Intuitive flashes are signals to pay attention, discern behavioral patterns, further evaluate, consider more carefully and explore options. Do not disregard behavioral cues that may alert you to potential problems before marriage.

Before marriage we should keep both eyes open. After marriage keeping one eye shut and being gracious to overlook flaws is a good idea.

Life is not the way it is supposed to be. It is the way it is. The way you cope with it makes the difference.

Learning how to properly cope with problems is extremely important to ensure your personal well-being and a happy ongoing marriage.

Keep things in perspective and remember to value people over possessions. Problems continually come in all shapes and sizes. Learn how to laughingly live with them and love the precious people around you despite the daily irritants.

Don't expect to change someone after marriage. It simply does not happen. You can't teach an old dog new tricks - at least not easily.

Find a dog that suits your fancy and until you do keep looking. What you tolerate will eventually dominate. You can have more in life if you don't settle for less.

Remember what you refuse to confront, you will never correct. Don't get angry with someone if you have never addressed such issues. There can be no assumptions. Make time for heartfelt discussion and decisions.

Questions to Ask Yourself and Others

1. Are there any specific set of behaviors you consistently want to operate out of in your life?
2. Are there any particular behaviors you want your future spouse to consistently do?
3. Are there any non-negotiables behaviorally that you will not live with or without? Some examples:
   "My wife must attend church with me."

   "My husband must take out the trash."

   "I will not live in another city."

4. What behaviors and habits do you want to eliminate or work on?

5. What behaviors will you commit to so as to maintain yourself physically?
6. What behaviors will you commit to so as to maintain yourself intellectually?
7. What behaviors will you commit to so as to maintain yourself spiritually?
8. What behaviors will you commit to so as to experience self-mastery and personal growth?
9. What will you continually do to honor and preserve your marriage?
10. What do you expect from your future spouse to assure you have a great marriage?
11. Does he or she cook?
12. Does he or she have a job? What kind?
13. What kind of social life do you desire after marriage? Will you continue to go out with friends or become a homebody?
15. What type of social life will you permit your future spouse to maintain after marriage? Can he keep going out with the boys? If so, what will he be permitted to do and not do? (i.e., strip clubs, dance clubs, shooting pool at the bar, ball games, men's meeting, dinner, car shows, etc.)

Remember what you refuse to confront, you will never correct. Don't get angry with someone if you have never addressed such issues. There can be no assumptions. Make time for heartfelt discussion and decisions.

Evaluate Environmental Issues

Environmental issues specifically mean things that surround you daily and affect your quality of life. Some people like four seasons, whereas others (such as myself) do not like cold weather unless they are snow skiing.

It behooves us therefore to know the personal preferences of someone before considering them for marriage. If they intend to live in a climate that gets terribly cold during winter, they may not be the ideal candidate for an islander or Floridian to marry.

Like it or not the weather affects all of our lives on a daily basis. If you do not think temperature and weather affects your quality of life than go to Siberia, Russia in the winter and see how you like it. Someone from a cold climate may not particularly care for south India in the summer where temperatures can be 110 degrees farenheit.

Other environmental issues to consider are existing children from previous marriages. Not everybody has the kindness and grace to accept children from former spouses. I know I certainly would not want to jump simultaneously into marriage and fatherhood in one day.

To someone deeply in love, kids from a former marriage could be counted additional bonuses. To others they might be seen sadly as excess baggage. People discussing marriage must honestly look at and consider all family involved.

I told my ex-wife that before we married that I would be taking care of my grandparents in their old age. I made it very clear up front that if this was something she was unwilling to do, than I was not the man for her. She graciously agreed that caring for my grandparents who raised me during my childhood was the right thing to do. Four years into our marriage when that time arrived, she selflessly assisted me in caring for both of my aging grandparents until they died. After they died, so too did my marriage which was concluded with a bitter divorce due to infidelity. Some things that are good for the family are not good for the marriage. All things must be considered.

Not everyone is so gracious and generous to embrace each other's extended family. The reality however is when you marry a person, you are also marrying into their family. Therefore you should make sure you like the family they come from because you will be spending time with them most likely every year.

My ex-wife had family strewn out across the country, whereas my family all lived in Florida. To visit my ex-wife's family I had to go on a national tour as she had siblings in Ohio, Massachusetts, Texas and Illinois. My ex-wife's mother lived in New York. Of course she wanted to see them all. Thankfully some of them had no problem coming to Florida in the winter to see her. The others who had jobs and limited income could not make the trip. I cannot emphasize it enough. Make sure you know who you are marrying and what family you are marrying into. These family issues will ultimately affect you. Once you sign up for marriage, there can be no looking back.

Most people do not consider such things before marriage. They are just in love or burning heavily with lust. Better than love at first sight is love with insight.

My cousin Corey in the U.S. Marines is happily married. He told me his game plan and strategy that he used prior to marriage. He had received some wise advice from a fellow Marine that told him: 'Marry a girl who has a college education and comes from a good family.'

Corey did so and says 'It worked like a charm.' Today he and the love of his life have a newborn baby boy and are as happy as can be.

Let me tell you, nothing is worse than being stuck with somebody whose family you despise or begrudge being with. It is not fair to either person as everybody deserves time with their family. Family moments are to be celebrated and shared equally once you are married.

Bickering over where to spend the holidays and with whom to visit during your vacations can be a real drain on your precious energy. Marry someone who you like to be with and who has a family you equally enjoy spending time with. Otherwise it is going to be a long haul for both of you and there will be a lot of friction along the way.

It is better to endure and patiently wait for someone who has all of your requirements than to settle for less and be forever aggravated after marriage. I would much rather be single and happy with me, than married to someone whose family I abhor and consider a bore.

Pets are another environmental issue to consider. I am somewhat allergic to cats and particularly don't care for their hair all over the place. I recall staying with one family that had three cats and I often found cat hair in my food. This may be o.k. for some, but it is not how I intend to live my life.

If you have fallen in love with a kitty cat lover and you are allergic to felines, you might want to pray that God heals you of your allergy or touches your future bride-to-be's heart to get rid of her cats. Otherwise you might want to have the local pharmacist get you some meds to help you through the feline frenzy.

Karla's cat Molly was a rare breed called a ragdoll that has rabbit-like fur. I didn't suffer too badly around her hair, but did find it a bit difficult when wearing black with Molly's hair. Though I happily invited Karla to bring Molly along to Florida, Karla wisely gave Molly to a friend as she knew we'd be traveling extensively.

Health issues are other things to consider. If your spouse has breathing problems, living in a congested city with pollution might not be the ideal place. Some people like myself require daily visits to a local health club for exercise. If the place you are considering living after marriage has no health club you might want to consider locating elsewhere, purchasing a home gym or modifying your workouts.

Some things are non-negotiables, which we do not want to give up. One young lady whom I was dating did not want to get rid of her cat which she had committed to care for. Incidentally she and the cat had to go. Fortunately we parted ways with a mutual understanding that we were 'just different.'

The cat was a deal breaker for me, but for some it would not be. You have to assess your own requirements and willingness to compromise and cooperatively work together. Be sure however to acknowledge and verbalize your non-negotiables up front so there are no surprises after the wedding day.

Geographical concerns are worthy of mention. Some prefer the country over the city. Others could not imagine being outside the city where everything is accessible. Do you prefer the mountains or the beach? Talk about where you want and expect to live after marriage. Where would your dream home be located?

Does he or she snore while they are sleeping. Certainly something like this can affect your quality of life. A nightly disturbance that disrupts and negatively affects your sleeping patterns can hinder the productivity of your entire life. This is not to say snoring is a deal-breaker, but definitely something to consider and account for. Such environmental issues, which we commonly overlook once they are upon us can be very troublesome. It is far better to know about and prepare for such challenges than to have them come upon you unawares.

Karla showed her unconditional love for me by enduring my snoring whenever I fell asleep on the couch with her. We later learned that I do well asleep as long as I'm on my side. Put me on my back however and I can suck the paint off of the walls during sleep.

Food preferences are another thing worthy of discussion. Karla and I both love Thai and Asian cuisine. I have never been so fortunate in my past relationships as most have not had a taste for international cuisine. As a man who has traveled the world, variety is important to me as I fully know what the earth has to offer. Thankfully Karla and I both eat healthy and enjoy variety. A boring and bland diet is definitely not for me. Yet to find someone with my exact tastes with whom to live was a miracle indeed. We both even like the same kinds of sauces, dressings and desserts. Taste and see the Lord is good!

How about the proximity of in-laws. Will they be living next door or in the same neighborhood? If so, how frequently will you be seeing them? Is his mother a busybody who has no life but always wants to interfere and poke her nose in yours? Such things should be considered since irritating relatives can be a nuisance and drain on a marriage.

Test & Evaluate Situational Circumstances

Some things are not tangible and visible, but they are most significant to your quality of life. First of all is the person's attitude and disposition. This can change like the wind for some people based on their surroundings, situational circumstances and workload.

Such elements and variables should be accounted for, but more importantly is for you to gauge whether your future spouse lives under their circumstances or rises above them. Attitude still determines altitude.

Until life's pressure is heavily applied you may not see all there is to know about yourself and your future mate. Once in the crucible of life things suddenly appear and surface which are worthy of acknowledging and closely examining. It is when things rub us the wrong way that what is deep within comes out for all to see. Anyone can happily carry on when all is going as planned and expected. It is during the hard times however that we are tested and to be inspected.

Key Points Review

Environmental issues specifically are things that surround you daily and affect your quality of life.

Know the personal preferences of someone before considering them for marriage.

Some things that are good for the family are not good for the marriage. All things must be considered.

The reality however is when you marry a person, you are also marrying into their family. Therefore you should make sure you like the family they come from because you will be spending time with them most likely every year.

Make sure you know who you are marrying and what family you are marrying into. These family issues will ultimately affect you.

Better than love at first sight is love with insight.

Marry someone who you like to be with and who has a family you equally enjoy spending time with. It is better to be single and happy, than married to someone whose family you abhor and consider a bore.

It is better to endure and patiently wait for someone who has all of your requirements than to settle for less and be forever aggravated after marriage.

Food preferences are another thing worthy of discussion. You might want to make sure your diets are complementary lest you torment each other in the kitchen and at meals.

Some people's disposition changes like the wind based on their surroundings, situational circumstances and workload.

Attitude still determines altitude. What attitudes are you willing to live with?

Until life's pressure is heavily applied you may not see all there is to know about yourself and your future mate.

Once in the crucible of life things suddenly appear and surface which are worthy of acknowledging and closely examining. It is when things rub us the wrong way that what is deep within comes out for all to see.

Anyone can happily carry on when all is going as planned and expected. It is during the hard times however that we are tested and to be inspected.

Love unconditionally, feel deeply, give wholeheartedly and forgive graciously.

Questions to Ask Yourself and Others

- Does he or she come from a good family?

- Do you like and get along with their family?

- Are there anything you dislike about this persons family?

- Are you ready to spend your holidays and vacation time with this person's family every year?

- Would you be willing to have this person's parents watch your children and instill their values and beliefs?

- Do you like this person's friends?

- Would you be willing to spend a night a week with this person's friends?

- Do you trust this person's friends to be a good influence upon them when you are not around?

- Do you like where this person lives?

- Would you be willing to relocate and move to their home?

- How well do they keep their house?

- Is their home a place you feel at rest and comfortable in?

- Does this person have children or other family com-mitments that would affect your life if you married them?

- Is this person people-oriented or do they tend to like their privacy and space? How would that affect you being married to them?

- To what extent do you want to allow friends and the extended family into your lives after marriage?

- Where do you want to live once you are married?

- What role models and positive examples does this person have in their life?

- What do you think about their role models and examples?

- How do they perform under pressure?

- How do they handle pain, sickness and discomfort?

- What is their work history?

- Do they get along well with people?

- Are they performance oriented or relationally motivated?

- Do they have a good report with those in the community?

- Do they have a Pastor, community leader or someone who would attest to their character?

- Are they punctual or do they tend to be late?

- Who else do you expect to be involved in this person's life and thus your life if you married them? How does that make you feel?

After making a positive change, we often allow others in our environment who have not changed their image of us. Don't allow others old image of you to anchor and hold you back into previous behavioral patterns. Your self-image does not need to revolve around others poorly updated understanding of you.

You are the master of your destiny. Your past reality is not your destiny. Humbly purpose to be all you can be. Commit to personal growth. Embrace change and persevere into the future. Your best and blessed days are ahead of you.

Prayer for Divine Relationships

I would like to take a moment to pray with you. It is my desire that you find true love and meaningful relationship. Please pray this heartfelt prayer here below out loud with your mouth making it your own.

"Dear God I thank you for wonderfully and uniquely creating me in your image. I acknowledge I am a social being that likes relationship and deeply yearns for true love. I humbly realize that I don't know it all and need Your help and guidance. Sometimes I err and fail relationally. Please forgive me for hurting people and heal me from the hurts I have experienced myself. Remove the unrealistic expectations I have placed on human beings. Help me to trust in you my Creator. I believe Your Son Jesus was sent to earth to die for humanity and reconcile mankind relationally.

Come Lord Jesus and empower me with your love, wisdom and power. As you rose from the dead, enable and empower me to rise above my past relationally failures. Blessed

Jesus, please fill me with Your Holy Spirit so I can love unconditionally, feel deeply, give wholeheartedly and forgive graciously. Come Holy Spirit and make my life what it ought to be. Bring about divine relationship and true love for me. Help me to love myself. Help me to love others. Help me dear God to know how much you love me. Let your love overtake and abound in my life from this day forward. In Jesus' Name. Amen."

If you prayed the above prayer, I would like to know about it. Please write me so we can together rejoice in your new commitment to live a life of unconditional love. You are important to me.

Your feedback, testimonies as to how this book has helped you, and insight as to how this book might be further improved are most welcomed. I would like to partner together with you to help humanity and make the world a better place to live. Write me today so we can become further acquainted, partner for dream fulfillment and support one another.

Best wishes as you live your dreams and pursue true love.

About the Author

Paul Davis is a worldwide professional speaker, life coach, and minister empowering people to live their dreams. A master in the art of communication and neurolinguistic programming, Paul has received extensive academic training and spiritual impartation from the best and the brightest. A highly sought after professional speaker, Paul's messages inspire, revive, awaken, impregnate with purpose, impart the fire of desire, catapult people into a new level of self-awareness, facilitate destiny discovery and dream fulfillment.

Paul has served many from working at ground zero during 9/11, serving in impoverished and tsunami stricken regions of the earth, and addressing audiences in war-torn nations. A minister of love, wisdom and power to the peoples of the world, Paul Davis breaks the mold, builds the individual, co-creates with you a compelling future to catapult you forward, enabling you to discover your intended destiny and fulfill your lifelong dreams!

Paul is a masterful poet and prolific author of several books including his pre-9/11 book *A State of Emergency*; *Breakthrough for a Broken Heart*; *Waves of God*; *Stop Lusting & Start Living*; *Supernatural Fire*; *God vs. Religion*; *Poems That Propel the Planet*; *Almighty Matchmaker* and many more!

Paul is a brilliant innovator, visual demonstrator and ingenious communicator. Paul possesses an uncanny ability to get beneath the layers of deception and denial, address the root problems inherent within an individual or organization while altering their perception, reconstructing their reality, renewing their vitality and moving them forth unto fulfilling their destiny.

Academically outstanding, Paul has collected degrees and certificates of completion from the University of Central Florida, Spirit Life Bible College, U. of Washington, Harvard Business School, Hofstra Law School, Hong Kong Law School and Reid & Associates in Advanced Interrogation. He is also Master Practitioner in NLP and Human Design Engineering. Paul excels in Communication, Negotiation, Transformative Mediation (Conflict Resolution), Counseling and Coaching. A Certified Fitness Trainer, Life Coach, and Licensed Minister — Paul is well equipped to fully develop a person's spirit, soul and body.

If you have unfulfilled dreams and longings of the heart that have yet to be realized, let Paul help you to pierce through your self-imposed limitations, pioneer a new path and passionately go after your dreams with a ferocious unstoppable passion! Bold and fearless, Paul has risked his own life for the results he has produced in the lives of others. Paul has defied natural law going to war-torn countries and nations on the brink of destruction to deliver his message. Indeed this man is the message.

Paul & Karla Davis can be contacted for Professional Speaking, Consulting, Coaching (professional & relational), Conflict Resolution, Restoring Order (professional organizing) and much more!

Paul & Karla Davis
Dream-Maker Inc.
PO Box 684
Goldenrod, FL 32733 USA
407-284-1705; 407-967-7553
RevivingNations@yahoo.com
www.DreamMakerMinistries.com
www.CreativeCommunications.TV
www.PaulnKarla.com
www.itietheknot.com

www.ingramcontent.com/pod-product-compliance
Lightning Source LLC
LaVergne TN
LVHW041116110825
818365LV00014B/688